Topsy and Tim

CHOCOLATE
COOK BOOK

Jean Adamson

BLACKIE: GLASGOW AND LONDON

Topsy and Tim always . . .

Wash their hands before they start cooking.

Put on their pinafores.

Wash up when they have finished.

Copyright © 1983
Jean Adamson

British Library Cataloguing in Publication Data
Adamson, Jean
Topsy and Tim's chocolate cook book
I. Title
823′.914 J   PZ7

ISBN 0-216-91363-2
ISBN 0-216-91362-4 (Pbk)

Blackie and Son Limited
Bishopbriggs, Glasgow G64 2NZ
Furnival House, 14–18 High Holborn, London WC1V 6BX

Printed and Bound in Great Britain

Topsy and Tim
always

always`

always

Ask a grown-up to melt the chocolate.

SAFETY FIRST

Topsy and Tim
like chocolate.
Who doesn't?

They like to cook
too. This is a book
of Topsy and Tim's
favourite chocolate recipes.

The step by step
pictures are easy
to follow—with
a little help
from a grown-up.

Chocolate Charlies

ALL YOU NEED to make seven
or eight Chocolate Charlies
is one 60 g bar of Cadbury's
Dairy Milk chocolate.

1 60 g chocolate...	**2** ...broken in a basin.	**3** Stand basin in a pan of water.	**4** Ask Mummy to melt chocolate.

USE A TEASPOON

5
Stir until smooth and runny.

6
Drop a blob on greaseproof paper . . .

7
. . . about as big as a 2p piece.

8
Dribble a body . . .

9
. . . and two legs . . .

10
. . . and two arms.

11
Fatten him up.

12
Give him some friends.

13
Leave them to harden.

Topsy's Chocolate CRISPIES

Easy to make

ALL YOU NEED IS
100 g Cadbury's Dairy Milk chocolate
and a big cup of Rice Krispies.

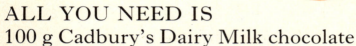

1 100 g chocolate..	**2** . . . broken in a basin.	**3** Stand basin in a pan of water.	**4**  Ask Dad to melt chocolate.
5 Add a big cup of Rice Krispies.	**6**  STIR WELL.	**7** Make little heaps on grease-proof paper.	**8**  Leave to set. Makes 10.

Tim's
Chocolate
CRUNCHIES

Quick setting

YOU NEED a big cup of cornflakes and 1 tablespoon each of Cadbury's Bournville cocoa, golden syrup, butter and sugar.

1
1 tablespoon butter in a pan.

2
Add 1 tablespoon golden syrup (warm spoon).

3
Add 1 tablespoon sugar.

4
Add 1 tablespoon cocoa powder.

5
Ask Mummy to melt them together.

6
STIR WELL.

7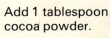
Add a big cup of cornflakes. Mix well.

8
Spoon into paper cake-cases.

9
Leave to set. Makes 10.

NUTTY NOSH

It's full of good things

50 g Bournville Dark
Plain chocolate
2 tablespoons each
of golden syrup
and butter or margarine

10 digestive biscuits
2 tablespoons each
of chopped nuts
and raisins
6 glacé cherries

FIRST the choc-mix

1 50 g chocolate . . .

2 . . . broken in a basin.

3 Add 2 tablespoons butter or margarine

4 and 2 tablespoons golden syrup.

5 Stand basin in a pan of water.

6 Ask a grown-up to melt it all together.

MEANWHILE
the biscuit mix

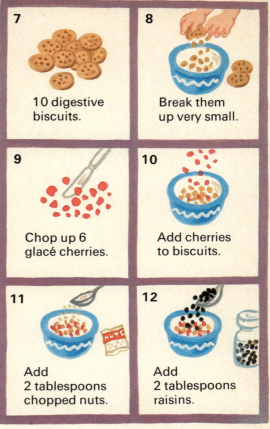

7
10 digestive biscuits.

8
Break them up very small.

9
Chop up 6 glacé cherries.

10
Add cherries to biscuits.

11
Add 2 tablespoons chopped nuts.

12
Add 2 tablespoons raisins.

LAST all mixed together

13
Stir hot-choc until smooth.

14
Add it to biscuit mix.

15
STIR WELL.

16
Put into a greased tin.

17
Press down. Leave to set.

18
Turn out and cut into squares.

Truffle MICE

YOU WILL NEED

100 g Bournville Dark Plain chocolate
Some liquorice boot laces and split almonds

2 tablespoons each of butter or margarine, orange juice or squash, icing sugar and ground almonds

1. 100 g chocolate (save 4 pieces) . . .

2. . . . broken in a basin.

3. Stand basin in a pan of water.

4. Ask Mummy to melt the chocolate.

5. Add 2 tablespoons butter or marg. Stir well.

6. Squeeze half an orange.

7. Add 2 tablespoons orange juice.

8. Add 2 table-spoons sifted icing sugar.

9. Add 2 tablespoons ground almonds.

10	11	12	13
MIX WELL.	Leave until firm—2 to 3 hours.	Roll into balls.	Grate 4 pieces chocolate, fine.
14	15	16	17
Coat balls in grated chocolate.	 Stick 2 split almonds in for ears.	 Snip pieces of liquorice bootlaces—	—for eyes, nose and tail.

Chocatop sand

YOU WILL NEED
1 tablespoon Cadbury's Bournville cocoa
2 tablespoons icing sugar
2 tablespoons soft margarine

1 Sift 2 tablespoons icing sugar.

2 Add 1 tablespoon cocoa.

3 Add 2 tablespoons soft marg.

4 Stir until smooth.

MAKE LOTS
AND STORE SOME
IN AN EMPTY
MARGARINE
TUB

...wich spread

1 Double Deckers

1	2	3	4
Choc-spread one slice of white bread.	Top with a slice of brown bread.	More choc-spread.	Make a double-decker.

2 Roly-Pops

1	2	3	4
Cut crusts off a slice of white bread.	Chocolate spread it.	Roll it up...	...cut it into little slices.

3 Sandwich Cake

1	2	3	4
 Choc-spread a sandwich cake.	More on top.	Grate some chocolate.	Sprinkle on top. Add dolly-mixtures.

LITTLE MONSTERS

YOU WILL NEED
Chocolate mini-rolls
A knob of soft margarine
1 teaspoon Cadbury's Bournville
cocoa
Dolly-mixtures
Cadbury's chocolate buttons

1 Take a knob of soft margarine.

2 Add 1 teaspoon cocoa.

3 MIX WELL to a paste.

4 Dip dolly-mixture nose in paste.

5 Stick on to end of roll.

6 Dip dolly-mixture eyes in paste.

7 Stick one on each side of head.

8 Break chocolate buttons in half.

9 Dip a half button in paste.

10 Stick on to little monster's back.

11 Stick another two on.

12 Make more.

EASTER NESTS

For NESTS you need
1 Shredded Wheat
100 g Cadbury's Dairy
Milk chocolate

1 Take 1 Shredded Wheat.	**2** Break it up.	**3** Take 100 g chocolate.	**4** Break it up in a basin.
5 Stand basin in a pan of water.	**6** Ask a grown-up to melt chocolate.	**7** Stir until smooth and runny.	**8** Add the Shredded Wheat.
9 MIX WELL.	**10** Put the mix in two heaps on a tin.	**11**  Shape nests with spoons.	**12**  LEAVE TO SET.

13

Sift 2 table-spoons icing sugar.

14

Add 2 teaspoons water. Make a STIFF mix.

15

Divide into 3 pieces.

16

Colour 1 piece blue.

17

Colour 1 piece pink.

18

Roll tiny eggs, 4 of each colour.

19
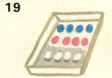
Leave to harden.

20

Fill nests with eggs.

Ice Chocalollies

For two lollies
YOU NEED
1 tablespoon Cadbury's
Drinking Chocolate
1 tablespoon hot water
1 orange

1

Put 1 tablespoon drinking chocolate in a cup.

2

Ask Mummy to add 1 tablespoon hot water.

3

STIR until creamy.

4

Squeeze an orange.

5

Add juice to drinking chocolate.

6

STIR well.

7

Fill two ice-lolly moulds.

8
Leave in freezer 2 hours.

Chocolate MILK SHAKES

For two milk shakes
YOU NEED
2 tablespoons Cadbury's
Drinking Chocolate
1 tablespoon hot water
2 cups milk

1 2 tablespoons drinking chocolate in a jug.

2 Ask Dad to add the hot water.

3 STIR until creamy.

4 Add 1 tablespoon ice-cream.

5 STIR until smooth and creamy.

6 Add 2 cups cold milk.

7 Whisk until frothy.

8 Serve with straws.

Chocolate
MONEY

ALL YOU NEED IS
40 g Cadbury's Dairy Milk chocolate
Two 2p pieces (well washed)
A little bit of plasticine
Some baking foil

1  Put plasticine on a 2p piece.	**2**  Stick another 2p on top.	**3**  Press baking foil over coins. Rub well.	**4** Now you have a coin mould. Make 12.
5  Take 40 g chocolate.	**6** Break it up in a cup.	**7** Stand cup in a pan of water.	**8** Ask Mummy to melt chocolate.
9  STIR until smooth and runny.	**10**  Put ½ teaspoon chocolate in each mould.	**11** Leave 5 mins. Smooth with knife.	**12** Leave ½ hour to set.

The tree ornaments are labelled: JOSY, stevie, Janet, Tony

13 Cut corners off foil.

14 Fold foil over chocolate coins.

15 Put coins in a net bag.

Oranges come in net bags. Ask Mummy to save the nets

Dad's favourite
BEFORE FOUR MINTS

YOU WILL NEED
100 g Bournville Dark Plain chocolate
5 heaped tablespoons icing sugar
1 tablespoon water
$\frac{1}{2}$ teaspoon peppermint flavouring
3 drops of green food colouring

1 The chocolate base

1 Take half the chocolate.	**2** Break it up in a basin.	**3** Stand basin in a pan of water.	**4** Ask Dad to melt chocolate.
5 Stir until smooth and runny.	**6** Pour on to greaseproof paper.	**7** Spread thin as a penny.	**8** Leave to harden.

2 The minty middle

1  Take 5 heaped tablespoons icing sugar.	**2** Sift into a basin.
3  Add 1 tablespoon water.	**4** Add ½ teaspoon peppermint.
5  Add 3 drops green food colouring.	**6** BEAT until smooth and stiff.
7 Spread evenly over chocolate.	**8**  Leave to set firm.

3 The chocolate top

1  Ask Dad to melt rest of chocolate.	**2**  Pour on to peppermint icing.
3 Spread smoothly all over.	**4** When set cut into pieces.

MUESLI MUNCH
Mummy's favourite

YOU WILL NEED
100 g Bournville Dark Plain chocolate
1 tablespoon golden syrup
1 tablespoon butter
6 heaped tablespoons muesli

1 Take 100 g chocolate.

2 Break it up in a pan.

3 Add 1 tablespoon golden syrup. Warm spoon first.

4 Add 1 tablespoon butter.

5 Ask Mummy to melt them gently.

6 Add 6 heaped tablespoons muesli. STIR well.

7 Put in a greased tin. Press flat.

8 Leave to set. Cut into pieces.